Changing Geography of the 20th Century

Dona Herweck Rice

Contributing Author

Ross D. Hudson

Consultant

Jennifer M. Lopez, NBCT, M.S.Ed.
Teacher Specialist—History/Social Studies
Office of Curriculum & Instruction
Norfolk Public Schools

Publishing Credits

Rachelle Cracchiolo, M.S.Ed., *Publisher*
Conni Medina, M.A.Ed., *Editor in Chief*
Emily R. Smith, M.A.Ed., *Content Director*
Véronique Bos, *Creative Director*
Robin Erickson, *Art Director*
Michelle Jovin, M.A., *Associate Editor*
Kevin Panter, *Senior Graphic Designer*

Image Credits: front cover (top), p.1 Library of Congress [LC-USF34-037392-D]; front cover (bottom), p.1 John Reps Papers, #15-2-1101. Division of Rare and Manuscript Collections, Cornell University Library; p.4 Popperfoto/Getty Images; p.5 (right), p. 11 (all), p.13 (top left and right), p.17 (center left), p.29 (bottom) U.S. National Archives; pp.6–7 Pinn Hans/AFP/Getty Images; p.8 (bottom) Hulton-Deutsch Collection/Corbis via Getty Images; p.9 (top right) LOC [LC-USZ62-39907]; p.9 (bottom) Newscom; p.10 (left) Reuters/Newscom; p.12 (top) LOC [LC-USZ62-126386]; p.12 (bottom right) U.S. Army [captured photo]; p.14 (left) Official photo by Y. Khaldey; p.14 (right) World History Archive/Alamy; p.15 (top) RIA Novosti Archive; p.16, p.19 Everett Historical/Shutterstock; p.17 (top right) Frame from US Government film "Duck and Cover"; p.18 (left) Veterans Administration; p.18 (right) Bernard Hoffman/The LIFE Picture Collection/Getty Images; p.20 (right) H. Armstrong Roberts/ClassicStock/Getty Images; p.21 (bottom) Yvonne Hemsey/Getty Images; p.22 (left) Kelly Miller/U.S. Army; p.22 (right) LOC [LC-DIG-fsa-8c02701]; p.23 (center left) LOC [LC-USW33-028633-C]; p.23 (bottom) LOC, William P. Gottlieb Collection; p.24 Joe Raedle/Getty Images; p.25 (left) Kit Leong/Shutterstock; p.27 (top) egd/Shutterstock; p.29 (top) JT Vintage/Glasshouse Images/Newscom; all other images from iStock and/or Shutterstock.

TCM Teacher Created Materials
5301 Oceanus Drive
Huntington Beach, CA 92649-1030
www.tcmpub.com
ISBN 978-1-4258-5073-9

Printed in China 51497

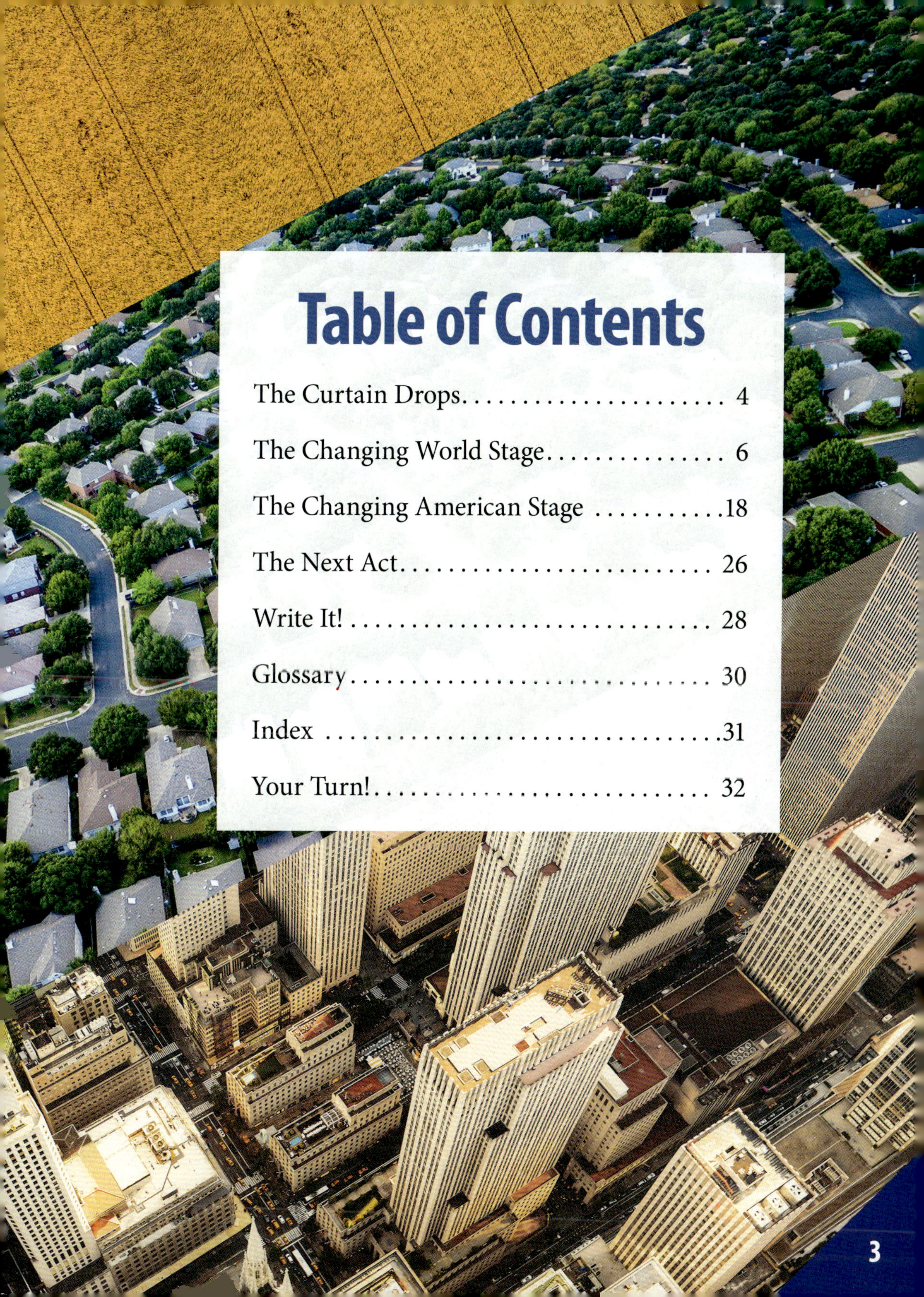

Table of Contents

The Curtain Drops

On March 5, 1946, the people of Fulton, Missouri, welcomed former British Prime Minister Winston Churchill. He had been a great leader during World War II. Now, he was in Fulton to speak about how the world was changing.

World War II was over. The Allied forces had won. People wondered what the world would look like after the war. Soviet Union leaders wanted to spread a form of government called **communism**. Under that system, the government controls the economy. This differs from much of the Western world. Many of these countries follow a system called **capitalism**. Under that system, people control the economy.

Churchill delivers his Iron Curtain speech in Fulton, Missouri.

Churchill's speech became known as the "Iron Curtain" speech. He said there was an imaginary curtain dividing Europe. One side was controlled by the Soviet Union. The other side was influenced by Western powers. The United States was on the Western side. The differing ideas on each side of the curtain created a strong political conflict. This conflict became known as the Cold War.

These years saw great change. World geography shifted. Different political powers rose up around the world. And the United States became a **superpower**.

Pearl Harbor

In 1941, pilots from Japan bombed a U.S. naval base. The base is called Pearl Harbor and is in Hawai'i. This attack pushed the United States into World War II. It also sparked U.S. involvement in world issues.

What Did He Say?

Churchill's speech made clear that the Cold War had begun. He said, "An iron curtain has descended across the Continent. Behind that line lie all the capitals of the ancient states of Central and Eastern Europe.... All these famous cities and the populations around them lie in what I must call the Soviet sphere."

The Changing World Stage

Israel

Israel used to be part of Palestine. Israel was declared an independent state in May 1948. However, challenges have continued there ever since. The Jewish, Christian, and Muslim religions all consider the land to be holy. No one wishes to give up its hold. They have not always found ways to share it peacefully.

Refugees

After World War II, there were around 10 million refugees in Europe. *Refugees* are people who flee from their home countries because they are not safe. They may not want to leave their homes, and they may face dangers on their travels. But they think the risks of leaving are worth it compared to the risks they face at home.

World War II caused the geography of the world to change. Many countries split apart, joined together, or changed their borders. Millions of people had died in events leading up to and throughout the war. That caused huge shifts in population. Other people moved to new places in large **migrations**. Many of these people were refugees seeking better lives.

▼ Jewish immigrants arrive in Palestine in October 1947.

Jewish People

In Europe, Jewish people were among those whose lives were dramatically changed by the war. Millions of Jewish people were killed in the Holocaust. The German government was mostly responsible for the Holocaust. German leaders had claimed that Jewish people were lesser. They took mothers, fathers, children, and more from their homes and sent them to **concentration camps**. These camps were prisons. Many times, German officials murdered the people in the camps.

In the months leading up to the Holocaust, Jewish people searched for safe places to live. Many people came to the United States. Then, after the war, the nation of Israel was established. Hundreds of thousands of Jewish people moved to the new nation. Another big migration came after 1989. This was when the Soviet Union broke apart. People were free to leave its borders, and many people moved to Israel.

China

In the 1930s, Japanese troops invaded many countries, including China. Years later, the Chinese government entered World War II to defend its borders. Half of World War II was fought in the Pacific. China played a key role in that war and helped to weaken Japan's military. This led directly to Japan's downfall. Together, the United States and China were victorious.

Fourteen million Chinese people were killed during the war. This caused a huge change in population. Then, after the war, a new leader rose to power. Mao Zedong—also known as Chairman Mao—led a communist takeover in China. Many people did not want to live in his People's Republic of China. So, they migrated.

pro-communism poster with Chairman Mao at the top

Chinese soldiers fire upon Japanese troops to stop their invasion into China. ▼

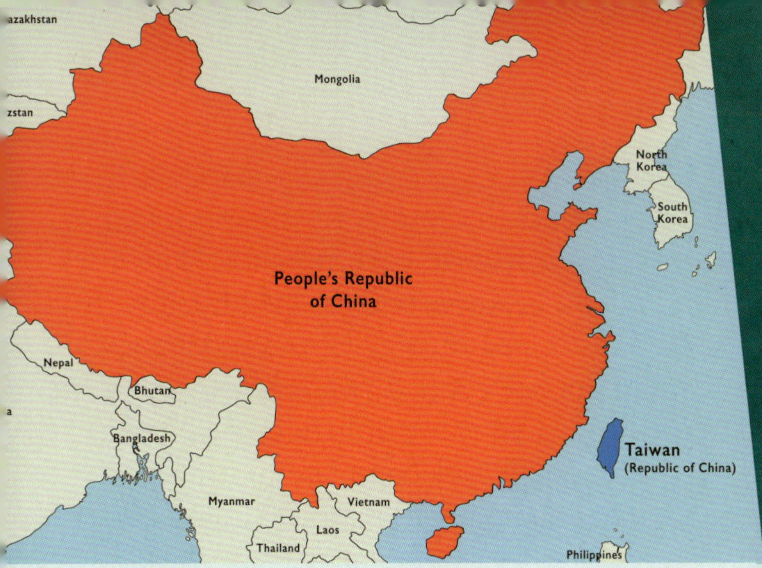

Millions of people went to Taiwan. Its population rose sharply during the twentieth century. It went from having 3 million people to having 22 million people. Other people went to the United States. This was a big deal. At the end of the nineteenth century, many Chinese people had found work in the United States. This rise in **immigration** led to a rise in anti-Chinese feelings. So, the U.S. government stopped all Chinese immigration. Then, Chinese people and Chinese Americans played a huge role in World War II. This changed how people felt. In 1943, the law was changed. People from China could immigrate again.

People in New York City's Chinatown celebrate the end of World War II.

Conflict in Taiwan

Chairman Mao's main rival was Chiang Kai-shek (shown above). When Zedong rose to power, Kai-shek and about two million of his supporters fled to Taiwan. Both Zedong and Kai-shek agreed that Taiwan was part of China. However, they disagreed over who was in charge. Kai-shek claimed that Taiwan was the true government of China. This debate still continues. Some people in Taiwan want to unite under the government of the People's Republic of China. Other people want Taiwan to become its own nation.

Ancient China

China is one of the oldest countries in the world. Its written history dates back nearly four thousand years. It has seen many forms of government throughout its long existence.

Korea

In the early twentieth century, Russia was invading parts of Japan. The Korean government let Japan set up a military base in Korea to fight the invasion. In the end, Japan stopped Russia. However, Japanese troops would not leave Korea. Korea's emperor asked for foreign help. This move only tightened Japan's hold. In 1910, Japan took complete control of Korea. As a result, many Koreans fled the country.

In time, the Korean people had had enough. Two million Koreans marched in a peaceful **protest** against Japan's authority. However, they were violently shut down. The country fell under total military rule. This rule lasted for 35 years, until Japan's defeat in World War II.

Assimilation

When the Japanese government was in charge of Korea, they practiced forced assimilation. They made all people speak Japanese. They changed how schools were run. Much of the land owned by Koreans was taken and sold to Japanese people. Forced assimilation like this takes away everything that makes a culture unique. It becomes just like another group.

Worlds Apart

When the Korean War ended in 1953, two nations formed. North Korea is communist. South Korea is democratic. The two countries have existed separately since then. However in recent years, leaders have worked toward building closer relations. In 2018, both sides made world news. The North Korean leader went to a meeting in South Korea. That was the first time a North Korean leader had gone south since the nation split in two.

After the war, the Soviet Union sent troops to the northern part of Korea. U.S. troops entered the southern part of Korea. Both sides were there to make sure Japan left. However, they had other goals too. The Soviets supported the establishment of a new government in the north. It would follow communism. In the south, the United States helped form a new government too. This one would be a democracy. As tensions rose, northern soldiers invaded the south. After three years, both sides signed a peace **treaty**. The settlement outlined new borders for North Korea and South Korea. The once-united country had broken in two.

U.S. soldiers during the Korean War ▶

▲ U.S. and North Korean leaders sign the peace treaty to end the Korean War.

Vietnam

For a century, Vietnam was under French rule. Many Vietnamese people did not want to be under French control. They wanted to be independent. One of those people was Ho Chi Minh. Ho was a rebel leader in Vietnam. He spoke in favor of an independent communist nation. Then, during World War II, Japan invaded Vietnam. Ho now had to get rid of two invaders.

After Japan lost the war, Ho declared that Vietnam was an independent nation. The French government tried to take back control of Vietnam, but Ho's side won. The peace treaty split Vietnam in half, with people in North Vietnam choosing Ho as their leader (a communist). The people of South Vietnam chose Ngo Dinh Diem (a democratic leader).

pro-communist soldiers during the Vietnam War ▼

U.S. soldiers during the Vietnam War

As Vietnam divided, the Cold War was in full force. The United States was fiercely opposed to the spread of communism. The U.S. government sent money and troops to support South Vietnam. By 1967, half a million U.S. troops had been sent. Battles raged on land, at sea, and in the air.

The effects of the Vietnam War were devastating. Refugees fled battle zones, looking for safety. Many Americans protested U.S. involvement in Vietnam. In 1973, President Richard Nixon withdrew U.S. armed forces. North Vietnam claimed full victory two years later. By that time, two million Vietnamese people had been killed. Twelve million people were refugees. The next year, the two nations came together to form the Socialist Republic of Vietnam.

Protests

The average age of American military members in the Vietnam War was 22 years old. As time went on, news stations began showing videos from Vietnam. People saw the horrors young people were facing. Protests were common, especially among young people on college campuses. A huge number of the young men who were **drafted** "dodged" the draft. Others fled the country.

Domino Effect

During the Cold War, the U.S. government worried about a domino effect. They thought that one country "falling" to communism would affect another country. It too would fall, and so on, like dominos. This fear was a key motivation for U.S. involvement in Vietnam.

Soviet Leaders

Vladimir Lenin was the first leader of the Soviet Union. After Lenin came Joseph Stalin (shown above). He was in charge for nearly 30 years, including during World War II. At the height of the Cold War, Nikita Khrushchev was placed in charge. Mikhail Gorbachev was the last leader of the Soviet Union.

McCarthyism

As the fear of communism spread, so did the panic about it. A U.S. senator, Joseph McCarthy, led a movement to rid the United States of communists. He especially went after people who worked in film and television. Many people were accused and investigated with little proof. They were encouraged to turn in other people as well. Many people were "blacklisted" from working, meaning no one would or could hire them. Their lives were ruined.

Lenin speaks to a crowd during the Russian Revolution.

The Soviet Union

World War I began in 1914. People from Russia were sent to fight in the war. That included farmers. With fewer farmers left in Russia, there was not enough food. More than five million people starved to death. So, in 1917, people began protesting against the government and the war. With that, the Russian Revolution began. It lasted for five years and ended with the creation of the Union of Soviet Socialist Republics, or the Soviet Union. The Soviet Union spread across northern Europe and Asia. It covered a huge area of land. In fact, it was about two-and-a-half times as large as the United States. However, the two governments were very different. The Soviet Union was a communist nation. The United States fought communism.

Soviet soldiers during World War II

During World War II, Germany invaded the Soviet Union. The Soviet people fought back. In the end, they played a key role in victory for the Allied forces. The war may not have been won without their efforts. The Soviet people paid a high price for this win. Around 20 million Soviet people lost their lives as a result of World War II.

This massive loss of life was not the only source of grief for the Soviets. The rise of the iron curtain meant a lot of struggling Soviet people could not receive help from the West.

The U.S. military tests a nuclear weapon in 1951.

The Soviet Union and the United States were both part of the Allied forces during World War II. After the war, however, tensions rose between the two nations. The countries entered the Cold War. This was not a war in the usual sense. It was a time of heightened tension. The Cold War was based on differing **ideologies**. It was also a fight for world power. The United States and the Soviet Union competed to be the best. They explored space and threatened each other with **nuclear war**. People were nervous about what each side would do next. The countries entered a kind of **stalemate**, each concerned that the other side would follow through with their threat of nuclear war.

Near the end of the Cold War, Mikhail Gorbachev came to power in the Soviet Union. He was a new kind of leader. He was open to Western ideas and goods. Bit by bit, he tried to turn the Soviet Union away from communism. In 1990, he won the Nobel Peace Prize. In late 1991, the Soviet Union came to an end. Fifteen countries formed from the old Soviet empire.

The Cold War was over. The geography of Europe was completely changed. People who wanted to leave could do so. Many people did.

Bert the Turtle

In the 1950s, the threat of nuclear war seemed very real. A film by the U.S. government, starring Bert the Turtle, gave advice on how to respond to a nuclear attack. Schools also held drills to see how quickly kids could "duck and cover" under their desks, just as a turtle might hide in its shell.

Changing Nationality

A lot of things changed when the Soviet Union came to an end. One of those changes affected all 293 million people living there. These people were no longer Soviet citizens. They were now citizens of the new countries the union had broken into.

The Changing American Stage

The twentieth century was a time of change for the world. The United States also felt that change.

Postwar Boom

During World War II, people had to limit how much food they ate and the goods they used to help the war effort. People were ready to celebrate after the war. Goods were in high demand. **Manufacturing** became a key industry.

G.I. Bill

In 1944, Congress passed a law called the Servicemen's Readjustment Act. It is more commonly known as the G.I. Bill. This bill helps veterans rebuild their lives. They receive money to earn college degrees or get certified through vocational schools. The G.I. Bill also offers support for veterans' families.

Rust Belt

Manufacturing towns thrived through much of the century. But some factories fell into decline in the late 1970s. Many people lost their jobs. These towns became known as the Rust Belt. When the factories fell, entire communities did too.

Workers assemble cars in 1946.

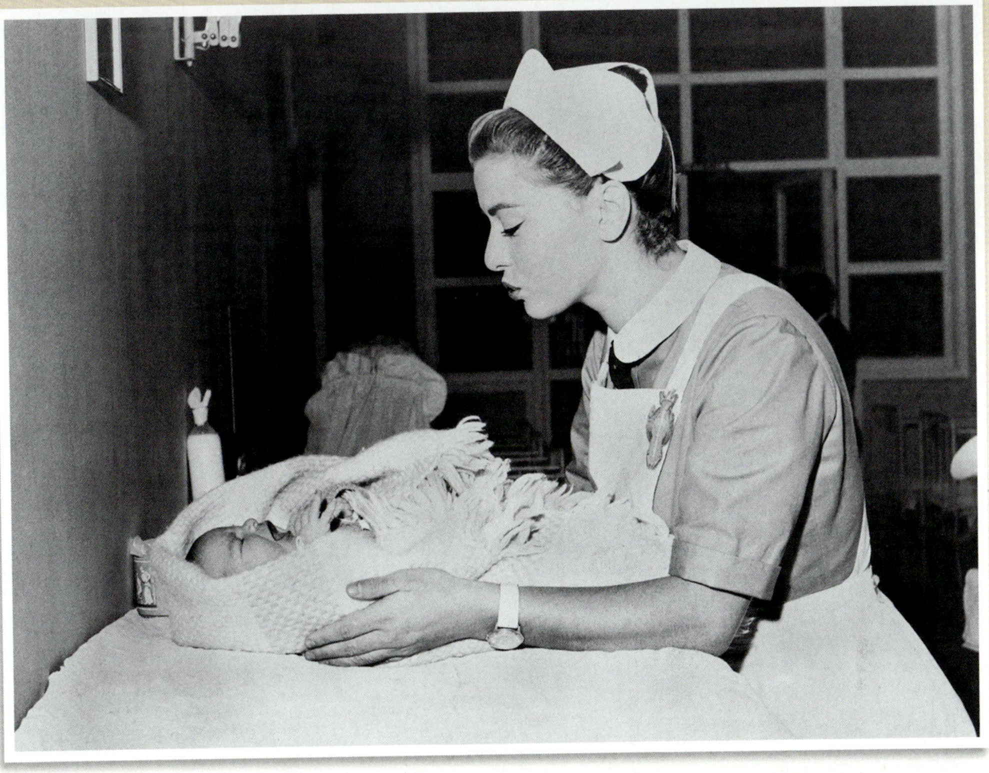

The shift from farming to manufacturing became more noticeable in the second half of the century. People moved to cities where these jobs could be found. Major manufacturing cities in the north, such as Detroit and Pittsburgh, grew quickly.

As the Cold War intensified, the U.S. government spent more and more money in the defense and space industries. Careers in these industries drew people south to cities such as Houston and Atlanta.

As the population shifted, it also grew. In the United States, between 1946 and 1964, there were around 76 million babies born! This time was known as the "baby boom." People who were born at that time are called *baby boomers*.

The baby boomer generation changed American life in many ways. They created new jobs. Unlike in the recent past, people were willing to treat themselves to **luxuries**. Americans rushed to buy new cars, television sets, and radios. They took vacations and explored new places. Americans were embracing new ways of life.

suburban housing development ▲

Welcome to the Suburbs

While many people moved to cities after World War II, other people did not want to live in cramped city apartments. Instead, they wanted space and homes of their own.

Welcome to the suburbs! The suburbs are groups of homes close to large cities. The suburbs offered mass-produced houses that many people could afford. Millions of people moved to the suburbs. As more and more people moved, new schools and other services were built. This inspired more people to move. This marked a major shift away from city life.

People created suburban communities across the country. California, Arizona, Texas, and Florida were popular states. They had plenty of open land and pleasant weather. Major industries also began to move. The West grew faster than any other region as industries changed and grew. Los Angeles in particular became a thriving city with a huge network of suburbs.

It was a time of growth, but booms never last. Increases in oil prices meant that manufacturing became more costly. A worldwide **recession** in the 1980s slowed government spending. Many people lost their jobs and could no longer afford to live in or near cities. Once again, people moved—this time to more **rural** areas. The geography of the nation changed again.

▼ People wait in lines at an unemployment office in 1982.

Fifty Nifty

As the population grew and changed, so did the country. Alaska and Hawai'i were added to the union in 1959. They became the 49th and 50th states. They were the first states to be added since Oklahoma, New Mexico, and Arizona. Those three territories became states in the early part of the century.

Lovely Levittown

The first suburbs were for the rich and upper-middle classes. One of the earliest suburbs for the growing middle class was Levittown. It was the first mass-produced, affordable housing development in the suburbs. It was built on old potato fields in Long Island, New York. The homes cost under $7,000. When the sales office opened, 1,400 homes were bought within the first three hours!

The Great Migration

For centuries, millions of black people were enslaved in the United States. Most enslaved people lived in the Southern part of the country. Some fled to freedom in the North. After the Civil War, all people were granted freedom. However, many black people still lived in poverty and fear.

The twentieth century was a time of change and growth for black people in the United States. Between 1916 and 1970, more than six million African American people left the rural South. This time was called the Great Migration. They went to cities in the Northeast, Midwest, and West. Half a million people moved to Chicago alone. They moved for jobs and for better lives. Racist laws in the South (called **Jim Crow laws**) made life hard. People looked for freedom and fairness. Moving to big cities gave people new opportunities as well.

After World War I

The first wave of the Great Migration came just after World War I. Many African Americans had served in the U.S. armed forces. After the war, they needed to find work. Factories were growing quickly in cities. A huge number of African Americans left their homes at this time to find better jobs and better pay.

Growth for All

The twentieth century was a time of growth and change for the nation. That growth included the U.S. economy. At the beginning of the century, there were 24 million workers. At the end of the century, there were 139 million workers.

▼ A group of people travel north during the Great Migration.

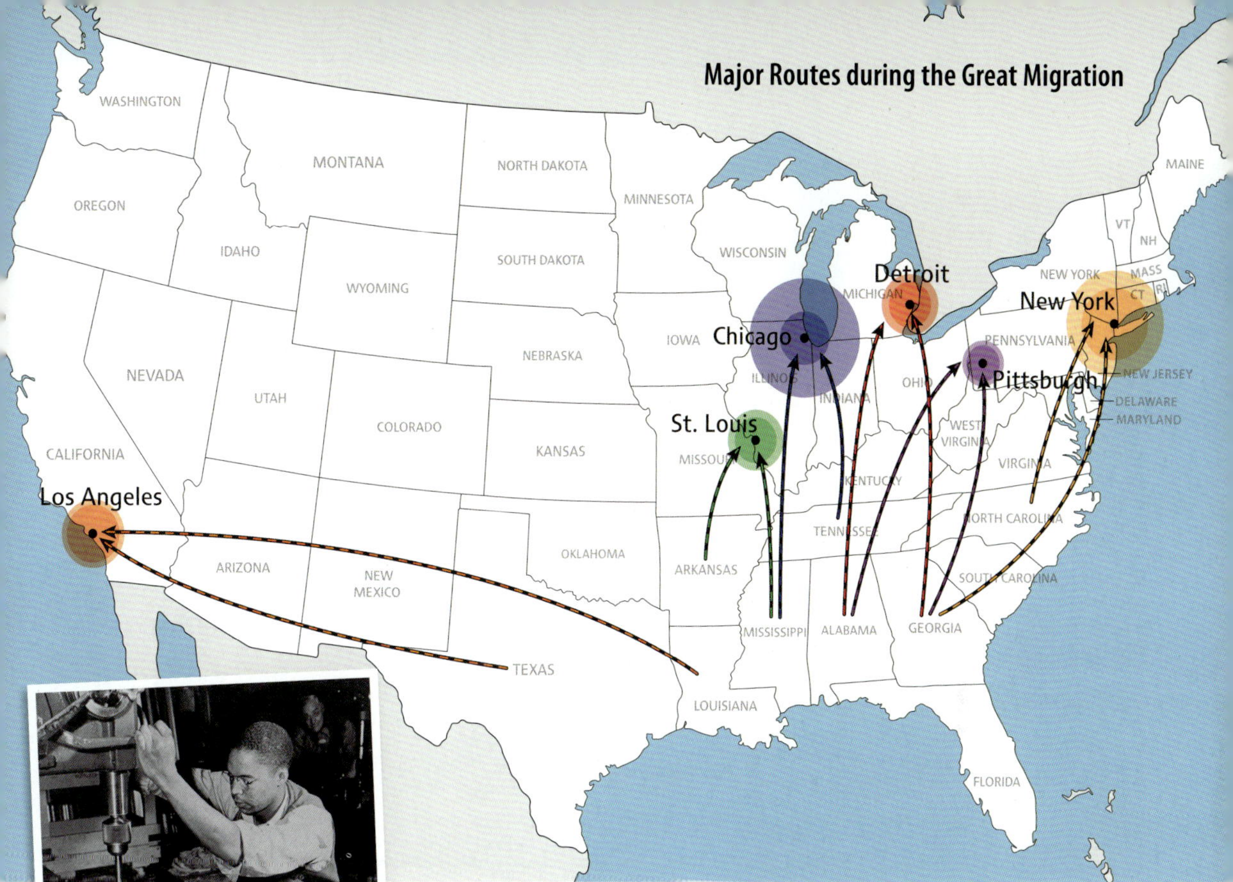

A worker assembles a plane in Los Angeles.

Harlem Renaissance celebrity Ella Fitzgerald sways to her music in New York in 1947.

Black people quickly established **urban** networks. Soon, black urban culture began to take hold. It was influential on American culture as a whole. The beginnings of this influence can be found in the Harlem Renaissance. This cultural awakening was based in Harlem, New York. Music, art, dance, and more developed and spread. The influence and effects of this renaissance continue to this day.

A group of immigrants becomes U.S. citizens. ▲

A New Home

The United States has a long history of immigration. Most people in the country can trace their ancestors back to another country. People still come. There are more than a million immigrants to the United States each year!

Millions of people moved to the United States after World War II. More than half were from Europe. A lot of those people had lost their homes in the war. The rate of European immigration slowed as countries improved from the war. At the same time, immigration from other countries rose as people escaped civil wars, poverty, and other issues. Many people felt they had to leave their home countries to stay safe. For much of the twentieth century, the United States served as a symbol of hope for people around the world.

Many immigrants first move to large cities, such as Los Angeles and Miami. Most major U.S. cities have **ethnic** sections. These places may have names like Chinatown or Little Italy. Immigrants may move to these places for their own comfort and ease.

About one in seven people living in the United States is a recent immigrant. Unlike most other countries, the United States has people with many cultures. Influences from around the world can be found all over the nation.

▼ a parade in Los Angeles's Chinatown section

Refugees

Refugees are sometimes called "asylum seekers." An *asylum* is a safe place. Each year, the president meets with Congress. As a group, they decide how many refugees will be allowed. The numbers change each year. Over the past 10 years, the United States has allowed around 70,000 refugees each year.

Online Population

In the beginning of the twentieth century, people had to live near their work. The introduction of cars, roads, and highways allowed people to live farther away. More recently, the internet has created another kind of commuter. Many people may live far away from their places of work because they can work online.

The Next Act

Population Growth

The growth of the world's population reached its peak in the 1960s. Since then, it has not grown at the same rate. However, the world is still growing very quickly. The world's population is expected to reach nearly 10 billion by the middle of this century.

Changing Labor Force

The U.S. labor force grew to be about six times as large at the end of the century as it was at the beginning of the century. The labor force changed in other ways too. New laws meant that there were no longer young children working. The number of farm workers went from almost 1 in 3 people in the United States to around 1 in 33. There were more women working outside their homes too. In 1900, 1 in 5 women were part of the workforce. In 1999, that was number was 3 in 5 women.

The geography of the world changed greatly during the twentieth century. However, it was not natural causes that created the biggest shifts. The main cause was people.

Country borders changed, and new ideologies took hold. The devastation of war forced people away from their homes. They tried to continue their lives elsewhere in safety and in peace. Within the United States, farm life shrank as city life grew. Less-populated parts of the country saw huge growth as people moved to cities and suburbs. Immigrants started new lives in the United States and changed the nation's culture.

When Churchill spoke of an iron curtain, he correctly predicted that the world was changing. He knew the world would look different at the end of the century from what it did at the start. The people of the world—living on both sides of the curtain—moved with the changing times. They hoped that the next move would bring a happy ending.

Write It!

So much of the past can be discovered through music. Many popular songs reflect people's experiences and histories. Bing Crosby's "I'll Be Home for Christmas" was written during World War II. It is meant to be a soldier's letter home to his family, in which he says he will return from war "…if only in my dreams." Marvin Gaye's "What's Going On?" was written after observing a violent protest during the Vietnam War. He looks at the violence and declares, "Brother, brother, brother / There's far too many of you dying." Sting's "Russians" is a Cold War era song meant to ask for peace in a time of tension. The singer cries, "There's no such thing as a winnable war."

Research historical songs and what they say about the times in which they were written. Then, think about the times you are living in now and what a song might say about them. Write lyrics to a song about current events or the current state of things. Just as with these other songs, be sure to have a clear point of view, message, or story in your song.

As an extra challenge, also write a melody for the song and sing it!

Welcome to the
JEANNETTE RANKIN PEACE PARADE
END THE WAR IN VIETNAM AND SOCIAL CRISIS AT HOME!

A
45 rpm
“WHAT'S GOING ON”
MARVIN GAYE

Glossary

capitalism—a system in which goods and production are privately owned

communism—a system in which all property is owned by the government

concentration camps—prisons where civilians are kept during wars

drafted—selected from the general population for military service

ethnic—relating to groups of people who have common traits and customs

ideologies—ideas representative of groups of people, nations, or political parties

immigration—the act of people coming to a country to live there

Jim Crow laws—acts that made it legal to separate groups of people based on race

luxuries—things people want but which are not necessary

manufacturing—refers to businesses that transform goods, materials, and substances into new products

migrations—groups of people who are moving from one place to another

nuclear war—a type of warfare that involves weapons powered by nuclear energy, which can cause major destruction

protest—an act that declares that someone is against something

recession—a period of time in which there is a decrease in economic activity and many people do not have jobs

rural—relating to a countryside area instead of a city

stalemate—a situation in which neither side can gain an advantage or win

superpower—an extremely powerful and influential country

treaty—an official agreement made between two or more countries or groups

urban—relating to cities instead of the countryside

Index

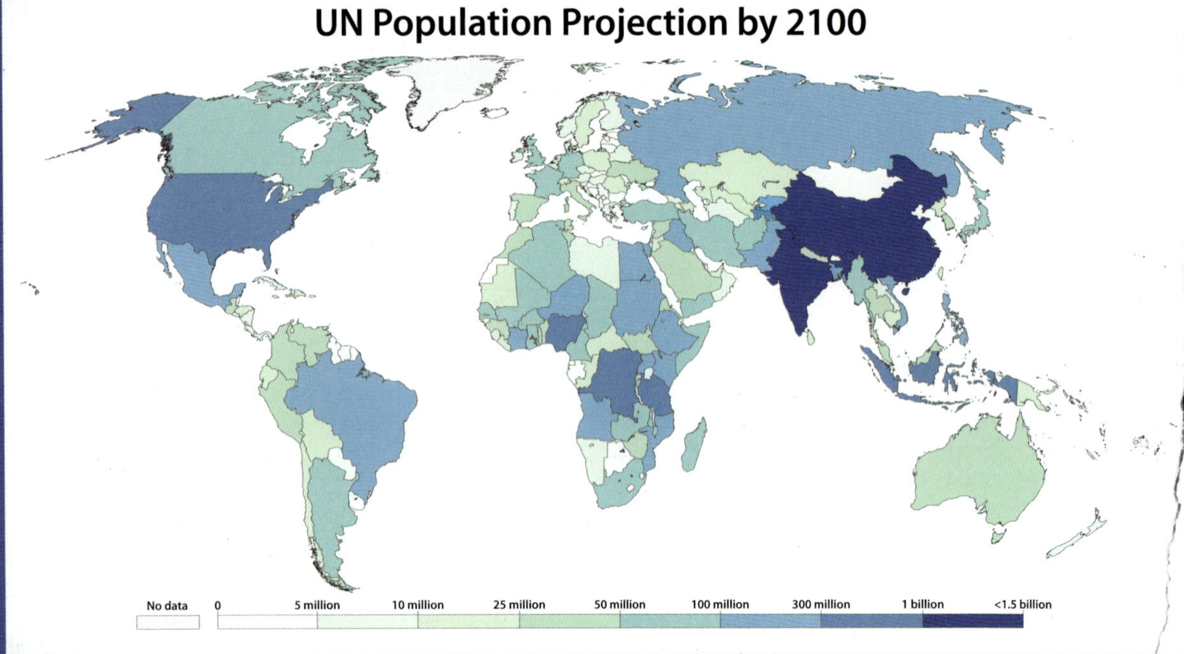

Your Turn!

The world's population continues to grow and change, just as it has done since the first humans walked the earth. People die, and people are born. They move to where they have the resources they need and are able to live the best lives they can. It has always been this way and likely always will be.

This map shows what the United Nations predicts will be the world's population by 2100. Places with darker colors are predicted to have higher populations. While the world's population continues to grow, the world itself does not. At some point, the number of people may reach beyond what the planet has room for. Certainly, the resources it can provide for people will reach a limit as well. Based on this map, write a description of what the world might be like in the year 2100.